BUGATTI
VEYRON

BY CALVIN CRUZ

TM

Are you ready to take it to the extreme?
Torque books thrust you into the action-packed world
of sports, vehicles, mystery, and adventure. These books
may include dirt, smoke, fire, and dangerous stunts.
WARNING: read at your own risk.

This edition first published in 2016 by Bellwether Media, Inc.

No part of this publication may be reproduced in whole or in part without written permission of the publisher.
For information regarding permission, write to Bellwether Media, Inc., Attention: Permissions Department,
5357 Penn Avenue South, Minneapolis, MN 55419.

Library of Congress Cataloging-in-Publication Data

Cruz, Calvin, author.
  Bugatti Veyron / by Calvin Cruz.
    pages cm -- (Torque. Car crazy)
  Summary: "Engaging images accompany information about the Bugatti Veyron. The combination of high-
interest subject matter and light text is intended for students in grades 3 through 7"--Provided by publisher.
  Includes bibliographical references and index.
  Audience: 7-12.
  Audience: Grades 3-7.
  ISBN 978-1-62617-279-1 (hardcover : alk. paper)
  1. Bugatti automobile--Juvenile literature. I. Title.
  TL215.B82C78 2016
  629.222'2--dc23
                              2015005751

TABLE OF CONTENTS

BUILT FOR SPEED

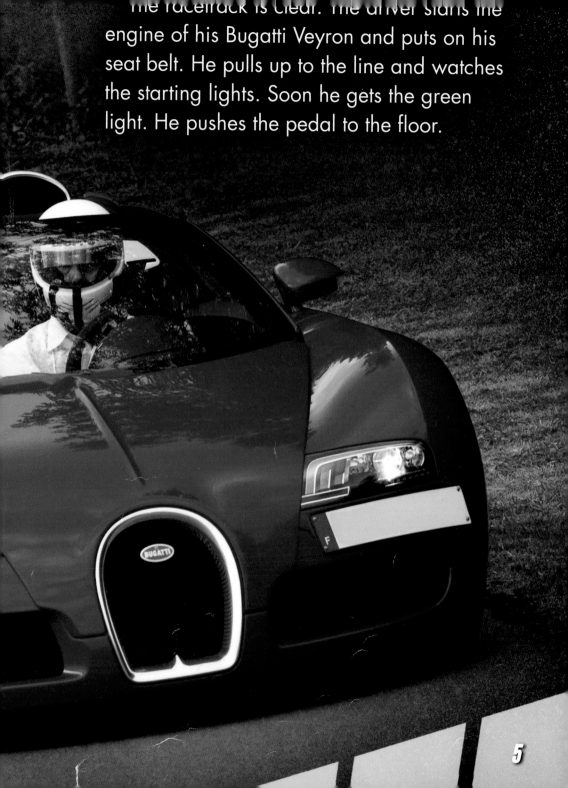

The racetrack is clear. The driver starts the engine of his Bugatti Veyron and puts on his seat belt. He pulls up to the line and watches the starting lights. Soon he gets the green light. He pushes the pedal to the floor.

The engine roars as the Veyron **accelerates**
down the track. Within seconds, it is going
almost 60 miles (97 kilometers) per hour!
The car comes around for another lap.
It has set a new track record!

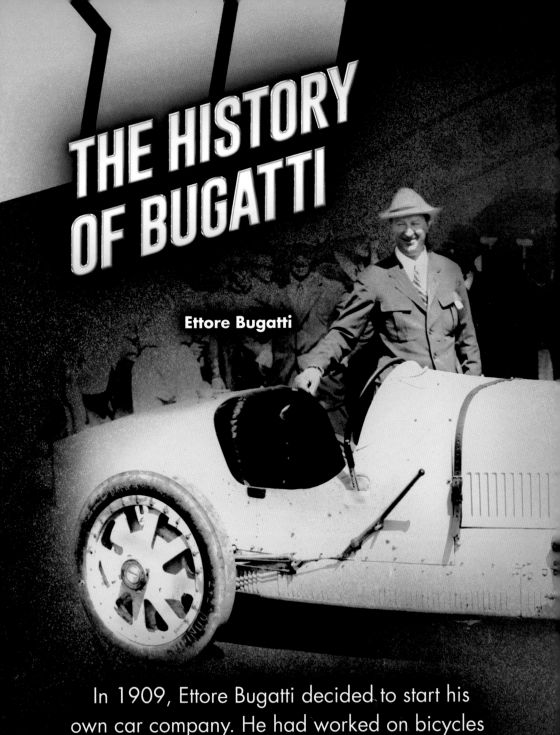

THE HISTORY OF BUGATTI

Ettore Bugatti

In 1909, Ettore Bugatti decided to start his own car company. He had worked on bicycles and cars for many years. Now he wanted more control over his car designs.

Ettore made cars that looked great and raced well. Throughout the 1920s and 1930s his cars won many **Grand Prix** races. In 1937 and 1939, Bugatti cars won the **24 Hours of Le Mans**.

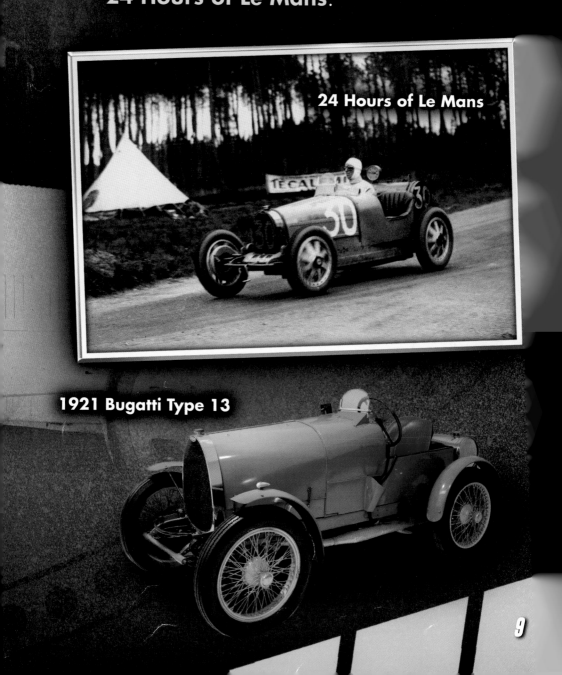

24 Hours of Le Mans

1921 Bugatti Type 13

Bugatti cars were popular but very expensive. The company struggled during the **Great Depression**. It started working on trains and airplane engines. By the 1950s, the Bugatti company had stopped making cars.

Bugatti railcar

ZZ₁ 24408

1931 Bugatti Type 46

Later, other companies bought the Bugatti
name. One company made parts for airplanes.
Another made more Bugatti sports cars.
In 1998, the Volkswagen Group bought
the Bugatti name. Bugatti cars have been
popular ever since!

BUGATTI VEYRON

Bugatti introduced the Veyron in 2005. It has the same focus on design and speed as Ettore's first cars. The Veyron is one of the fastest **street legal** cars in the world! It can come as a **coupe** or as a **convertible**.

coupe

convertible

2013 Bugatti Veyron
16.4 Grand Sport Vitesse

BEST OF THE BEST
THE VEYRON WAS NAMED CAR OF THE DECADE FOR THE 2000s BY THE TELEVISION SHOW *TOP GEAR.*

TECHNOLOGY AND GEAR

The heart of the Veyron is its **W16 engine**. It has 16 **cylinders** arranged in the shape of a "W."

The Veyron has a simple **interior**. A leather and **aluminum** design gives the car a classy feel. It also has a top-of-the-line sound system. Its speakers were first designed to be used in homes!

W16 engine

A FORMULA FOR SPEED
THE VEYRON USES THE SAME ACCELERATION TECHNOLOGY AS FORMULA 1 RACE CARS!

spoiler

The Veyron is less than
4 feet (1.2 meters) tall. Its short
height makes it **aerodynamic**.
A movable **spoiler** helps the
car grip the road.

To keep the driver in control, the Veyron has powerful brakes. At high speeds, the spoiler tilts to become an **airbrake**. The Veyron can go from 248 miles (400 kilometers) per hour to a complete stop in less than 10 seconds!

TODAY AND THE FUTURE

The Veyron's speed and design have made it a fan favorite for more than ten years. More powerful editions of the Veyron have boosted its popularity. The Veyron Super Sport has broken many speed records!

2015 BUGATTI VEYRON SPECIFICATIONS

CAR STYLE	COUPE OR CONVERTIBLE
ENGINE	8.0L W16
TOP SPEED	254 MILES (409 KILOMETERS) PER HOUR
0 - 60 TIME	ABOUT 2.5 SECONDS
HORSEPOWER	1,001 HP (746 KILOWATTS) @ 6000 RPM
CURB WEIGHT	4,162 POUNDS (1,888 KILOGRAMS)
WIDTH	78.7 INCHES (200 CENTIMETERS)
LENGTH	175.7 INCHES (446 CENTIMETERS)
HEIGHT	45.6 INCHES (116 CENTIMETERS)
WHEEL SIZE	19.7 INCHES (50 CENTIMETERS) FRONT
	21 INCHES (54 CENTIMETERS) BACK
COST	STARTS AROUND $1,700,000

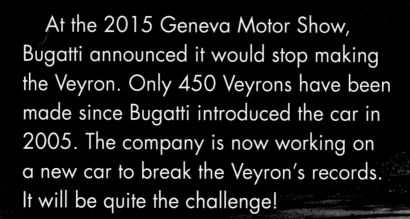

At the 2015 Geneva Motor Show, Bugatti announced it would stop making the Veyron. Only 450 Veyrons have been made since Bugatti introduced the car in 2005. The company is now working on a new car to break the Veyron's records. It will be quite the challenge!

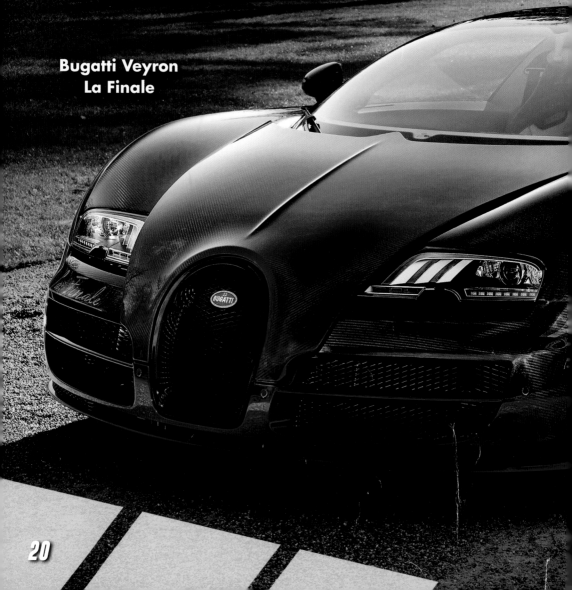

**Bugatti Veyron
La Finale**

CREST LINE ON THE HOOD   **SHORT HEIGHT**   **ROUNDED BODY**

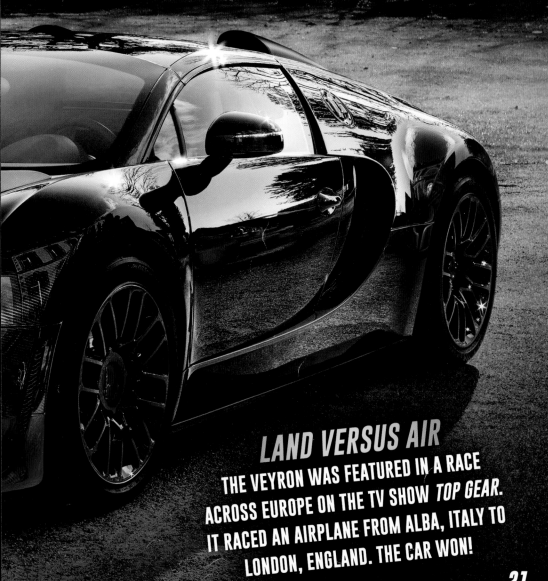

LAND VERSUS AIR

THE VEYRON WAS FEATURED IN A RACE ACROSS EUROPE ON THE TV SHOW *TOP GEAR*. IT RACED AN AIRPLANE FROM ALBA, ITALY TO LONDON, ENGLAND. THE CAR WON!

GLOSSARY

24 Hours of Le Mans—a race in which a team of drivers competes for 24 hours

accelerates—increases in speed

aerodynamic—having a shape that can move through air quickly

airbrake—a spoiler on the back of the car that is raised when the driver brakes

aluminum—a strong, lightweight metal

convertible—a car with a folding or soft roof

coupe—a car with a hard roof and two doors

cylinders—a chamber in an engine in which fuel is lit

Grand Prix—a high-level racing competition

Great Depression—a period of time from the late 1920s through the 1930s when people did not have a lot of money

interior—the inside of a car

spoiler—a part on the back of a car that helps the car grip the road

street legal—able to be driven on public roads

W16 engine—an engine with 16 cylinders arranged in the shape of a "W"

TO LEARN MORE

AT THE LIBRARY

Gifford, Clive. *Car Crazy*. New York, N.Y.: DK Publishing, 2012.

Hamilton, John. *Sports Cars*. Minneapolis, Minn.: ABDO Pub., 2013.

Kenney, Karen Latchana. *Thrilling Sports Cars*. North Mankato, Minn.: Capstone Press, 2015.

ON THE WEB

Learning more about the Bugatti Veyron is as easy as 1, 2, 3.

1. Go to www.factsurfer.com.

2. Enter "Bugatti Veyron" into the search box.

3. Click the "Surf" button and you will see a list of related web sites.

With factsurfer.com, finding more information is just a click away.

INDEX

The images in this book are reproduced through the courtesy of: GBAA/ ZOB/ ZDS WENN Photos/ Newscom, front cover; pbpgalleries/ Alamy, pp. 4-5, 17; Frank Hollis/ Alamy, pp. 6-7; Heritage Images/ Corbis, p. 8; adoc-photos/ Corbis, p. 9 (top); Gunold Brunbauer, p. 9 (bottom); Hemis/ Alamy, p. 10; Jörn Friederich/ Glow Images, p. 11; Darren Brode, p. 12 (top); Max Earey, p. 12 (bottom); Bugatti, pp. 13, 14-15, 16, 18, 20-21; VanderWolf Images, p. 19.